Oxford Read and Discover

Helping Around the World

Activity Book

Name: _____

Age: _____

Class: _____

School: _____

OXFORD
UNIVERSITY PRESS

OXFORD
UNIVERSITY PRESS

Great Clarendon Street, Oxford OX2 6DP

Oxford University Press is a department of the University of Oxford.
It furthers the University's objective of excellence in research, scholarship,
and education by publishing worldwide in

Oxford New York

Auckland Cape Town Dar es Salaam Hong Kong Karachi
Kuala Lumpur Madrid Melbourne Mexico City Nairobi
New Delhi Shanghai Taipei Toronto

With offices in

Argentina Austria Brazil Chile Czech Republic France Greece
Guatemala Hungary Italy Japan Poland Portugal Singapore
South Korea Switzerland Thailand Turkey Ukraine Vietnam

OXFORD and OXFORD ENGLISH are registered trade marks of
Oxford University Press in the UK and in certain other countries

© Oxford University Press 2011
The moral rights of the author have been asserted
Database right Oxford University Press (maker)
First published 2011
2015 2014 2013 2012 2011
10 9 8 7 6 5 4 3 2 1

No unauthorized photocopying

All rights reserved. No part of this publication may be reproduced,
stored in a retrieval system, or transmitted, in any form or by any means,
without the prior permission in writing of Oxford University Press,
or as expressly permitted by law, or under terms agreed with the appropriate
reprographics rights organization. Enquiries concerning reproduction outside
the scope of the above should be sent to the ELT Rights Department, Oxford
University Press, at the address above

You must not circulate this book in any other binding or cover
and you must impose this same condition on any acquirer

Any websites referred to in this publication are in the public domain and
their addresses are provided by Oxford University Press for information only.
Oxford University Press disclaims any responsibility for the content

ISBN: 978 0 19 464572 0

Printed in China
This book is printed on paper from certified and well-managed sources.

ACKNOWLEDGEMENTS

Helping Around the World Activity Book by: Alistair McCallum
Illustrations by: Kelly Kennedy, Dusan Pavlic/Beehive Illustration,
and Gary Swift

Introduction — Page 3

1 **Circle the correct words.**

1 People help each other in some **countries** / **all countries** / **one country**.

2 Doctors and teachers have jobs that help **animals** / **cars** / **people**.

3 Volunteers give their time **for money** / **freely** / **for food**.

4 Volunteers usually help **their friends** / **their family** / **many different people**.

5 **Doctors** / **Parents** / **Students** are usually paid for their work.

6 A veterinarian, or vet, is a doctor who cares for **children** / **old people** / **animals**.

2 **Answer the questions.**

1 Write four jobs that help others.

_____

_____

2 Are there volunteers in your country? What do they do?

_____

_____

3 Do you sometimes help other people? How?

_____

4 Which job would you like to do?

_____

 **Caring for Others**

1 **Write the words. Then complete the sentences.**

   ˢtⁿeˢtⁱd _____   ᵈⁱᵥⁱˢeₘw _____

   ʳeˢuⁿs _____   ᶜₒtdₛor _doctors_

   eᶜrª ˢwerrok _____ ᵍeₛⁿuʳₛo _____

   1 _Doctors_ find out why people are sick, and help them to get better.

   2 _____ do difficult operations.

   3 _____ give medication, and care for sick people and their families.

   4 _____ help to bring babies into the world.

   5 _____ care for people's teeth.

   6 _____ help people who are old, sick, or disabled.

2 **Order the words.**

   1 to / healthy. / important / It's / stay
      It's important to stay healthy.

   2 life. / save / to / It's / someone's / amazing
      _____

   3 stay / We / healthy. / help / to / can / ourselves
      _____

   4 voluntary / do / Anyone / work. / can
      _____

3 Match the halves of sentences.

1 Many people do jobs...   [d]
2 Workers like doctors and nurses...   [ ]
3 In some schools, there's a nurse...   [ ]
4 Doctors and nurses sometimes give vaccinations...   [ ]
5 If we eat well, and do sport, we probably...   [ ]
6 Hospice workers can help...   [ ]

a to help children who are sick.
b people a lot at the end of their life.
c so that people do not get serious diseases.
d that care for others.
e won't get sick very often.
f are very important.

4 Complete the sentences.

1 Doctors often work in c__linics__ or hospitals.
2 We can learn about being h_____ from doctors and nurses.
3 Other people can help us if we are sick or disabled, or if we have an a_____.
4 When people are going to die, they sometimes stay in a h_____.
5 Every year, about 130 million babies are b_____.
6 V_____ often give help after an emergency.

2 Teaching Others 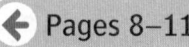 Pages 8–11

1 Write the words.

1 a rt____

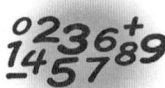

2 m_____

3 h_____

4 g_____

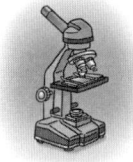

5 s_____

6 l_____

2 Match. Then write complete sentences.

school teachers have	just for children
education helps people	after college or university
many people can't	a very special job
education isn't	have a good education
professors need to know	a lot about their subject
education doesn't stop	to get a better job

1 School teachers have a very special job.

2 _____

3 _____

4 _____

5 _____

6 _____

3 Match the people with the sentences.

> trainers   parents   ~~classroom assistants~~   professors
> school teachers   cooks   playground assistants

1 They give more help to children who need it.
   classroom assistants

2 They help children to stay safe.
   _____

3 They teach at colleges and universities.
   _____

4 They help very young children to eat, walk, talk, and play.
   _____

5 They help workers to do their job better.
   _____

6 They teach children subjects like mathematics.
   _____

7 They make snacks and lunch for children and teachers.

4 Complete the sentences.

1 Teachers get _c h i l d r e n_ ready for _ _ _ _ _ life.

2 One of the most _ _ _ _ _ _ _ _ university _ _ _ _ _ _ _ _ is law.

3 _ _ _ _ _ _ _ _ _ _ doesn't stop after college or university.

3 Food for Everyone ← Pages 12–15

1 Write the words. Then complete the sentences.

negrad _____ xevesepin _____
rostm _____ rametsurepks _supermarkets_
defe _____ gebatvesel _____
hayhlet _____ satiders _____

1 _Supermarkets_ sell a lot of food.

2 _____ food helps people to stay well.

3 Some people have a _____ where they can grow fruit and _____.

4 Sometimes, people can't buy food because of a natural _____ like a bad _____.

5 Sometimes food is too _____, and people don't have enough money to _____ themselves and their families.

2 Circle the correct words.

1 In Asia, farmers grow a lot of **corn** / **rice**.

2 Almost 50% of the world's corn is grown in **North America** / **Brazil**.

3 Farmers grow **vegetables** / **fruits** like carrots and onions.

4 Around the world, about one **million** / **billion** people don't have enough food.

5 In some countries, **farmers** / **scientists** have learned to make rain.

3 Order the words. Then write *true* or *false*.

1 important / food / of / has / nutrients / lots. / Healthy
   <u>Healthy food has lots of important nutrients.</u>   <u>true</u>

2 the food / grow / eat. / most / Scientists / that / of / people
   _____   _____

3 Europe, / lot / a / farmers / of / rice. / grow / In
   _____   _____

4 cane / of / Brazil. / in / 30% / sugar / About / grown / is
   _____   _____

5 the / food / on / sell / Internet. / People
   _____   _____

4 Complete the sentences.

> crops   money   clouds   seeds   stores
> ~~charities~~   chemicals   farmers

1 Some <u>charities</u> give people _____, so that they can grow food.

2 Experienced farmers teach other _____ how to grow the strongest, healthiest _____.

3 Fairtrade farmers usually sell their crops straight to _____ and supermarkets, so that the farmers get more _____.

4 To make rain, scientists put special _____ into very cold _____.

4 Water for Everyone ← Pages 16–19

1 Write *industry*, *farming*, or *home*.

We use water…

1 to give to animals.   _farming_
2 to help machines to work.   _____
3 to wash ourselves.   _____
4 to grow crops.   _____
5 to flush the toilet.   _____
6 to make the things we need. _____

2 Correct the sentences.

1 People need dirty water to stay healthy.
   People need clean water to stay healthy.

2 Most of Earth's water is fresh water in the oceans.
   _____

3 Only about 10% of Earth's water can be used by people.
   _____

4 In some places, there isn't enough water, and this makes life easy.
   _____

5 People in poorer countries have all the clean water they need.
   _____

6 Today, there are about one billion people on our planet.
   _____

3 Match. Then write complete sentences.

everything on Earth	save	chemicals to clean dirty water
people	use	from rivers and lakes
people can	needs	clean water to drink
a billion people	build	water
we can all help to	comes	reservoirs to store water
a lot of fresh water	don't have	water

1 <u>Everything on Earth needs water.</u>

2 _____

3 _____

4 _____

5 _____

6 _____

4 Complete the sentences.

> don't take   put   don't use   take   don't fill   turn off

1 _____ too much water when you brush your teeth.

2 _____ the water when you have enough.

3 _____ water in the refrigerator.

4 _____ a shower.

5 _____ a bath.

6 If you have to take a bath, _____ the bathtub.

 **Helping in Emergencies**

1 **Complete the words. Then match with the sentences.**

1 d _i_ s _a_ st _e_ _r_   [d]
2 w _ _
3 e _ _ t _ qu _ ke
4 _ ef _ g _ e
5 c _ ar _ _ y
6 t _ un _ m _

a A person who has to leave their home or their country in an emergency.

b A giant wave that travels very fast.

c When the ground shakes, and buildings fall.

d Something very bad that damages Earth, people, or animals.

e When people or countries fight.

f A group of people who collect money to help other people.

2 **Order the words.**

1 people / very quickly. / emergencies, / need / In / help

_____

2 of / the world. / are / refugees / in / There / millions

_____

3 frightening / have / refugees / experiences. / Most / had

_____

4 to live. / need / Refugees / food, / somewhere / water, and

_____

5 to build / charities / camps. / help / refugee / Some

_____

3 Complete the questions. Then write answers.

> where ~~when~~ how many when what

1 __When__ do people become refugees?
   __When they leave their homes in an emergency.__

2 _____ do people need in emergencies?
   _____

3 _____ do refugees often live?
   _____

4 _____ people died in the tsunami in Indonesia?
   _____

5 _____ was there a huge earthquake in Haiti?
   _____

4 Complete the sentences.

1 Refugees try to help t_____, but this can be very d_____.
2 Refugees need to see a d_____ if they have been h_____ or if they are sick.
3 Charities help refugees to go back to their h_____ when it's s_____.
4 Earthquakes and tsunamis are terrible n_____ disasters.
5 After the Haiti earthquake, people made refugee c_____ for people who had l_____ their homes.

6 Caring for Animals Pages 24–27

1 Write the words.

1 c a t   2 _ _ _ _   3 _ _ _ _

4 _ _ _ _   5 _ _ _ _ _   6 _ _ _ _ _ _ _

7 _ _ _ _ _ - _ _ _ _   8 _ _ _ _ _ _ _ _ _ _ _

2 Complete the sentences.

> Indonesia   Pacific   Germany   Asia   Arctic

1 There are about 4,500 wild snow leopards in _____.

2 Some volunteers in _____ collect toads that are migrating near dangerous roads.

3 An animal charity in _____ helps young orang-utans.

4 Gray whales spend the summer in the cold _____ Ocean.

5 Gray whales swim to the warmer _____ Ocean in October.

3 Circle the correct words.

1 Vets care for **people** / **animals** / **buildings**.
2 Some people help young orang-utans when their parents have been killed by **hunters** / **doctors** / **charities**.
3 When orang-utans are older, they can return to the **city** / **ocean** / **forest** if it's safe.
4 Volunteers rescue animals that are hurt after disasters like **water** / **oil** / **sugar** spills.
5 Whales live in **rivers** / **lakes** / **oceans**.
6 Whales are very **heavy** / **dangerous** / **slow**.

4 Match the halves of sentences.

1 People take their pets to the vet…
2 Many people give money…
3 Birds that are covered in oil will die…
4 Whales often travel…
5 Some whales swim into water…
6 If whales can't get back to the deep ocean,…

a to animal charities.
b that isn't deep enough.
c if people don't clean them.
d they become very tired.
e when they are sick or hurt.
f thousands of kilometers every year.

 # Protecting Life on Earth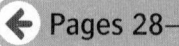

1 Complete the sentences.

> seeds hunters meat conservationists
> species medicines

1 There are many millions of _____ of plant and animal.
2 _____ work to protect species that are threatened.
3 We use some plants as _____.
4 Some charities care for young elephants when their parents have been killed by _____.
5 If we leave flowers, more plants will grow from the _____.
6 People have killed elephants for _____.

2 Order the words.

1 important / are / Species / ways. / many / in
   _____

2 extinct / every / 150 / More / day. / species / become / than
   _____

3 where / leave / flowers / grow. / should / We / always / they
   _____

4 threatened / WWF / to / species. / works / protect
   _____

5 individual / and animals / plants / die. / All
   _____

3 Match. Then write complete sentences.

all species	use	finding new species
people	eat	to help elephants
animal charities	need	plants as medicines
people	keep	each other
people have	try	land from elephants
scientists	taken	plants and animals

1 _____
2 _____
3 _____
4 _____
5 _____
6 _____

4 Complete the sentences.

1 When every plant or animal in a _ _ _ _ _ _ _ _ has died, the species is _ _ _ _ _ _ _ _.

2 In the USA, conservationists move sea turtle _ _ _ from busy beaches to quieter places where they can _ _ _ _ _ _ safely.

3 People and elephants have lived near _ _ _ _ other for thousands of _ _ _ _ _ _.

4 People have cut down trees and _ _ _ _ _ _ _ that elephants need for _ _ _ _ _.

8 Helping Our Planet ← Pages 32–35

1 Complete the sentences.

> climate   vehicles   crops   trees   planet   fossil

1 Everyone should care for our _____.
2 Pollution comes from _____ like cars and planes.
3 To make electricity, people burn _____ fuels like coal and oil.
4 Many scientists think that Earth's _____ is changing.
5 People cut down millions of _____ to clear land.
6 Farmers clear land so that they can grow _____ and keep animals.

2 Correct the sentences.

1 For thousands of years, there has been life on our planet.

_____

2 People help Earth with pollution that comes from cars and planes.

_____

3 When we make electricity, we make the Earth too cold.

_____

4 Many volunteers plant new trees before a fire.

_____

5 Today, most cars use gasoline that's made from water.

_____

3 Circle the correct words.

1 Many volunteers clean beaches after **a fire / an oil spill**.
2 Biogas can be made from **plants / coal**.
3 Scientists can make clean electricity from **oil / the sun**.
4 We **should / shouldn't** use very hot water to wash our clothes.
5 When we make lots of new things, we use lots of **carbon dioxide / electricity**.
6 When we aren't using the computer, we should turn it **off / on**.

4 Order the words. Then answer the questions.

1 our / care / planet? / we / Should / for
   Should we care for our planet?
   Yes, we should.

2 becoming / some / Are / hotter and drier? / countries
   _____
   _____

3 electricity / a lot / to / water? / use / we / of / heat / Do
   _____
   _____

4 fuels / Will / forever? / be / fossil / there
   _____
   _____

5 from / biogas / make / waste? / we / Can
   _____
   _____

# After Reading 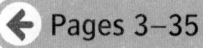 Pages 3–35

1. **Check your answers to Activity 1, page 3.**

   1 = all countries   2 = people   3 = freely
   4 = many different people   5 = Doctors   6 = animals

2. **Complete the puzzle.**

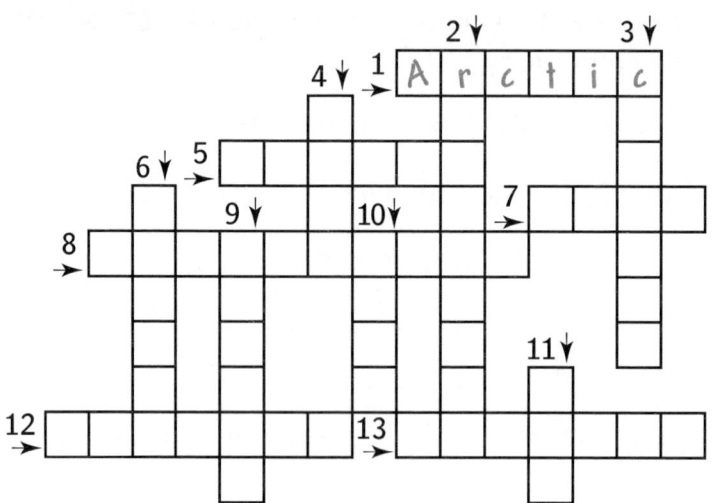

1. Gray whales spend the summer in the ___ ocean.
2. Fresh water can be stored in a ___.
3. Port-au-Prince is the ___ of Haiti.
4. ___ can rescue people after earthquakes.
5. ___ is a fuel that can be made from waste.
6. A lot of sugar cane is grown in ___.
7. Scientists can put chemicals into clouds to make ___.
8. ___ teach at colleges and universities.
9. Coal and oil are ___ fuels.
10. Water in the oceans is ___ water.
11. Gasoline is made from ___.
12. There are about six ___ people on Earth.
13. A ___ teaches workers new information.

3 Write the words. Then find and write the page.

1. This is a charity that works to protect threatened species all around the world. ___WWF___ _page 30_
2. Sometimes, people who are old, sick, or disabled live here. _____ _____
3. Almost 50% of the world's corn is grown here. _____ _____
4. Doctors or nurses give these so that people do not get serious diseases. _____ _____
5. People become these when they have to leave their home in an emergency. _____ _____
6. When we burn coal or oil, we make a lot of this. _____ _____
7. These are people who give their time freely to help others. _____ _____
8. We use this to wash clothes and flush the toilet. _____ _____
9. These people help to bring babies into the world. _____ _____
10. We use a lot of this to heat water. _____ _____
11. We should take this instead of a bath. _____ _____
12. Up to 200 of these become extinct every day. _____ _____

4 Complete the sentences. Use the words in the box and the verbs in parentheses.

> is   are   was   ~~is~~   were   are

1. Help <u>is needed</u> after an emergency. (need)
2. In 2007, more sugar cane _____ than any other crop. (grow)
3. Doctors and teachers _____ money for their work. (pay)
4. When a species is extinct, it _____ forever. (lose)
5. More than 250,000 homes _____ in the earthquake in Haiti. (damage)
6. Birds that _____ in oil will die if people don't clean them. (cover)

5 Complete the sentences.

> a lot   all   too   enough   very   too much

1. When we are _____ young, our parents help us to eat, walk, and talk.
2. You shouldn't use _____ water when you brush your teeth.
3. People in richer countries are lucky, because they have _____ the clean water that they need.
4. Some whales swim into water that isn't deep _____.
5. Professors need to know _____ about their subject.
6. In some places, people can't grow crops because the weather is _____ hot.

6 Complete the sentences with words from A, B, and C. Then complete the chart with your own sentences.

A help work ~~care~~ bring teach give get grow

B protect time problems babies food ~~people~~ workers ready

C ~~sick~~ adult eat freely threatened job pollution world

People	What do they do?
Doctors	They ___care___ for ___people___ who are ___sick___.
Midwives	They _____ _____ into the _____.
School teachers	They _____ children _____ for _____ life.
Trainers	They _____ _____ to do their _____ better.
Volunteers	They _____ their _____ _____.
Farmers	They _____ most of the _____ that people _____.
Conservationists	They _____ to _____ species that are _____.
Environmental campaigners	They _____ people about _____ like _____.
Vets	_____
Professors	_____

My Book Review

Title of this book: _____

Name of the author: _____

This book is about people who _____ others.

Questions about this book

1 What new words did you learn from this book? (Write six words.)
   _____
   _____

2 Write three jobs that help other people.
   _____

3 Which job is the most interesting?
   _____

4 Write two animals that are in the book.
   _____

What I like about this book

My favorite chapter was _____.

My favorite picture was _____.

My scores for this book (draw ☺, ☺☺, or ☺☺☺)

Interesting book ◯◯◯   Interesting cover ◯◯◯

Interesting pictures ◯◯◯   Fun to read ◯◯◯

Which book do you want to read next? _____